KimZ

Orchids
A Brief Exploration Through Art

An Adult Coloring Book
for the Artistic Expression of All

Author
Marcèle Tasse

Illustrations by
The Preeminent Kim Z

Colorization on Page I
Richard Eijkenbroek

Blue Reed Publishing
Wichita, Kansas
2015

FIRST EDITION

Printed in the USA

This Book is dedicated to the Loving Memory of
Mrs. Mildred Taylor
A Lover of Good Things...

About the Artists

Drawings

I'm Nguyen Kim Hoang Nhu, you can call me KimZ. I'm 23 years old, a full-time artist and Illustrator in Vietnam. My drawings take a lot of inspiration from nature and children. I love to draw illustrations for children's stories. You can see my website at kimzillu.com. Thank you.

Colorization on Page I

I am Richard Eijkenbroek. I am a Dutch graphic designer, illustrator and photographer, who's a logistics engineer in real life. I was born in 1978 and I find joy in exploring the world of art, experimenting with different techniques and styles. My painting tablet and a variety of painting programs are my canvas. "The object isn't to make art, it's to be in that wonderful state which makes art inevitable." — Robert Henri

● ● ● ● ●

This book was created with the adult in mind. The complexity of the drawings are meant to extend the propensity of adult creative expression and stimulate the artistic ingenuity of the experienced mind. It was designed as an indulgence, to provide hours of stress relief, peace, relaxation and pleasure to the partaker.
We hope you will enjoy bringing color and life to these wonderful works of art.

Purchasers of this title can receive a PDF copy of the coloring pages (for personal use only) for only $7.99. Proof of purchase is required. Email us your proof of purchase and we will send you a link to acquire the PDF file.

If you desire your pages be shipped to you please indicate this in your email along with your mailing address, an additional $0.99 shipping and handling fee will apply.

To order by mail include your payment, proof of purchase, an additional $0.99 shipping and handling fee and we will ship the pages to you.

Blue Reed Publishing
PO BOX 21454
Wichita, KS 67218
Orchids@bluereedpublishing.com

Orchids

A Brief Exploration Through Art

● ● ● ● ●

KimZ

KimZ

KimZ

KimZ

KimZ

KimZ

KimZ

The Orchidaceae, known by its common name "orchid" is a family of plant characterized by their bright beautiful flowers. The orchid boasts many unique traits and a rich history.

Did You Know?

- Orchids are an amazingly diverse, ancient species of flower.

- Orchids are found all over the world.

- The ancient Greeks used some types of orchids as aphrodisiacs.

- Orchids are one of the largest families of flowering plants. There are more than 25,000 species of orchids.

- Some species of orchids are used for medicinal purposes.

- Orchids have a symmetry similar to human faces.

- Vanilla is a species of orchid.

- Certain species of orchids are capable of living up to 100 years.

- There are orchid species whose flowers mimic certain insects, attracting them to pollinate.

- Orchids come in many different sizes ranging from very very small to hundreds of pounds.

- Orchid seeds are the smallest in the world.

- The term orchid is a fairly new term as it was not introduced until 1845.

Expand your experience, take the time to learn more about these fantastic alluring flowers.

Special thanks to all who made this book a reality.